All patterns in this book may be worked with Peyote Stitch or Brick Stitch. I personally bead the rectangular designs with Peyote Stitch. The only one I recommend Brick Stitch for is the Soaring Eagle pattern on page 18.

Basic Brick Stitch Instructions

Row one base row: Usually the middle or widest row is the base row unless indicated otherwise on the pattern. Pick up 2 beads on your needle and position them toward the end of the thread. Holding beads in place with your thumb and forefinger, run the needle through them again in same direction making a circle.

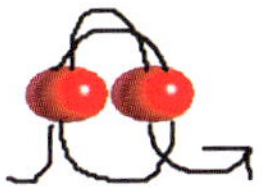
2

Pull the circle tight positioning the 2 beads side by side.

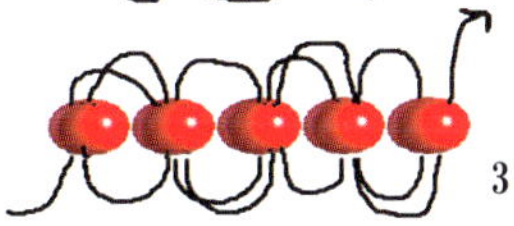
3

Continue adding more beads until you have the total you need for the base row.

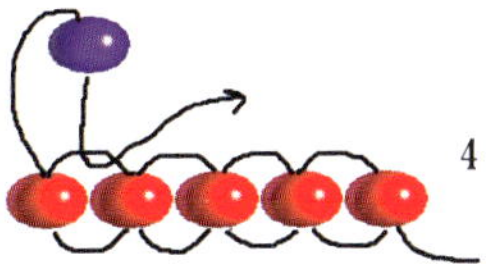
4

Turn work around. Always work from left to right. For the second row, with a bead on the thread, bring the needle through the top loop that goes between the last 2 beads of the very first row.

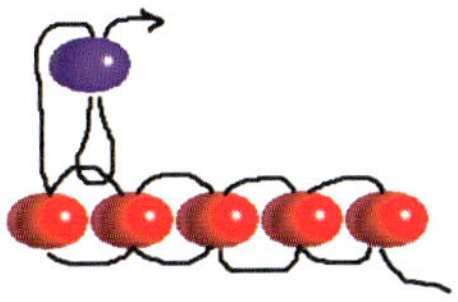
5

Pull the bead into place. Bring the needle back up through the bead coming up through the bottom and pull it down.

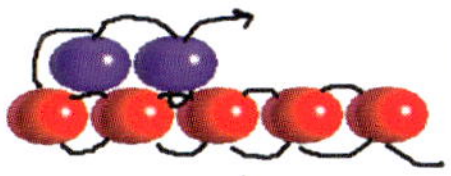
6

If the thread is pulled too tight, the beadwork becomes rigid and warped. Just pull up the slack until the bead is snug. Continue to add beads as shown to the end of the row.

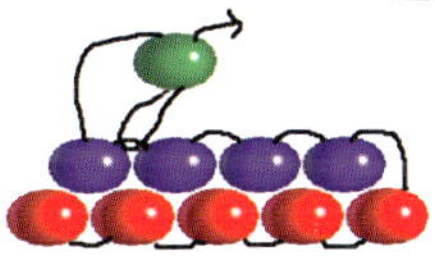
7

Turn and continue in the same manner for the remaining rows.

8

Weave the thread through the finished work and clip the thread close to the beads.

Joining Seams

To join a peyote stitch with a 'zipper' join, have both of your edges meet with the beads alternating on either side so they will interlock like a zipper. Take your thread through the first end bead, through the next bead that fits into the 'zipper' on the other side and continue this way, pulling on the thread every 3 or 4 stitches. Don't pull too tight or your work will warp.

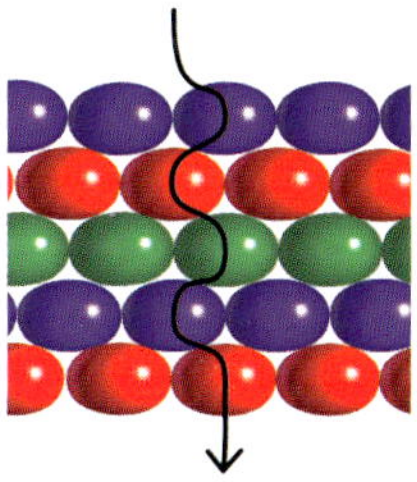

Ideas for Fringe

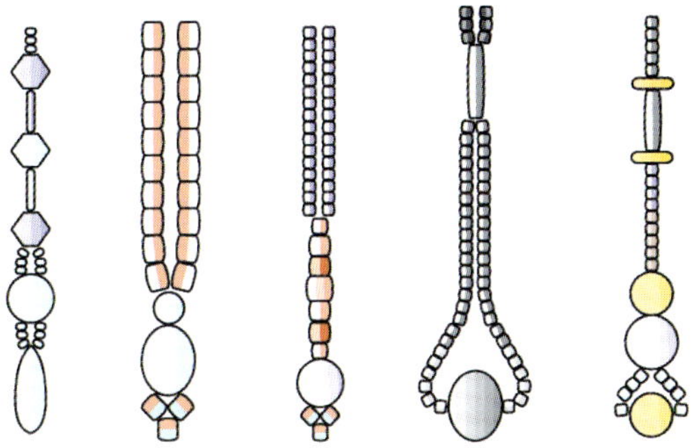

When you string the fringe, all the bead holes are facing down, so the strands of fringe will hang straight down from the bag, forming two side by side rows of thick fringe.

Alpha Wolf
Pages 4 - 5

Spirit Horse
Pages 6 - 7

The Bear Facts
Pages 8 - 9

Foxy
Pages 10 - 11

Winter's Teeth
Pages 12 - 13

Sundown
Pages 14 - 15

Desert Dusk
Pages 16 - 17

Soaring Eagle
Pages 18 - 19

Captured Dream
Pages 20 - 21

Four Directions
Pages 22 - 23

Indian Rug
Pages 24 - 25

Native Rug
Pages 26 - 27

Star Rug
Page 30 - 31

Kachina
Pages 28 -29

Sun Shines Woman
Pages 32 - 33

Contemplation
Pages 34 - 35

Alpha Wolf

Have fun finishing this wolf bag with natural stones, silver and other accents! Change the border colors to make him look completely different!

Bag by Deb Atkins
The Bead Hive, Wichita, KS 67213
316-264-6616, D7442039@aol.com
Fringe, feathers & strap by Tina Napier, jnapier3@cox.net

Stitch: Peyote or Brick | Size: Approximately 2 1/2" x 3" | Beads Used: Delica

Begin Here - work Peyote Stitch beginning with this row. Work from left to right across the pattern.

For straps and embellishments, gather your own collection of beads, natural stones and crystals. Plan a design that makes the bag uniquely yours. Note: The bead quantities given do not include fringe and strap.

- **#205** - Opaque Pearl Beige - 116 beads
- **#208** - Opaque Tan - 3 beads
- **#772** - Dyed Matte Transparent Mauve - 13 beads
- **#69** - Lined Rainbow Crystal Tan - 26 beads
- **#863** - Matte Rainbow Transparent Grey - 88 beads
- **#884** - Matte Opaque Rainbow Brown - 24 beads
- **#211** - Opaque Alabaster - 46 beads
- **#321** - Matte Metallic Silver - 292 beads
- **#230** - Lined Opalescent Crystal 24kt Gold - 43 beads
- **#411** - Galvanized Gold - 39 beads
- **#851** - Matte Rainbow Transparent Crystal - 20 beads
- **#336** - Matte Metallic Palladium Plated - 52 beads
- **#35** - Galvanized Silver - 146 beads
- **#52** - Lined Rainbow Crystal Ivory - 18 beads
- **#110** - Transparent Rainbow Ice Blue - 24 beads
- **#107** - Transparent Grey Iris - 23 beads
- **#301** - Matte Opaque Blue Grey - 176 beads
- **#306** - Matte Opaque Gunmetal - 119 beads
- **#307** - Matte Opaque Grey - 252 beads
- **#871** - Matte Opaque Rainbow Jet - 186 beads
- **#252** - Transparent Pearl Grey - 14 beads
- **#882** - Matte Rainbow Opaque Grey - 142 beads
- **#80** - Lined Rainbow Crystal Lavender - 47 beads
- **#231** - Lined Lustre Crystal White - 20 beads
- **#325** - Matte Metallic Iris Blue - 109 beads
- **#111** - Transparent Rainbow Black Diamond - 140 beads
- **#37** - Lined Metallic Crystal Copper - 92 beads

Spirit Horse

The horse is another fun pattern to embellish... What about making snaffle bit earrings or a bracelet using the strap pattern? Or add horseshoe nails, conchos or a fine braided leather strap. Change the colors in the border to make it match just about any piece in your wardrobe.

Lampwork Glass in Strap by Morebeads
beads@morebeads.com
Sample by Dawn Marvin, Mourning Dove Makings
mourndovemakes@hotmail.com

Stitch: Peyote or Brick

Size: Approximately $2^{1}/_{2}$" x 3"

Beads Used: Delica

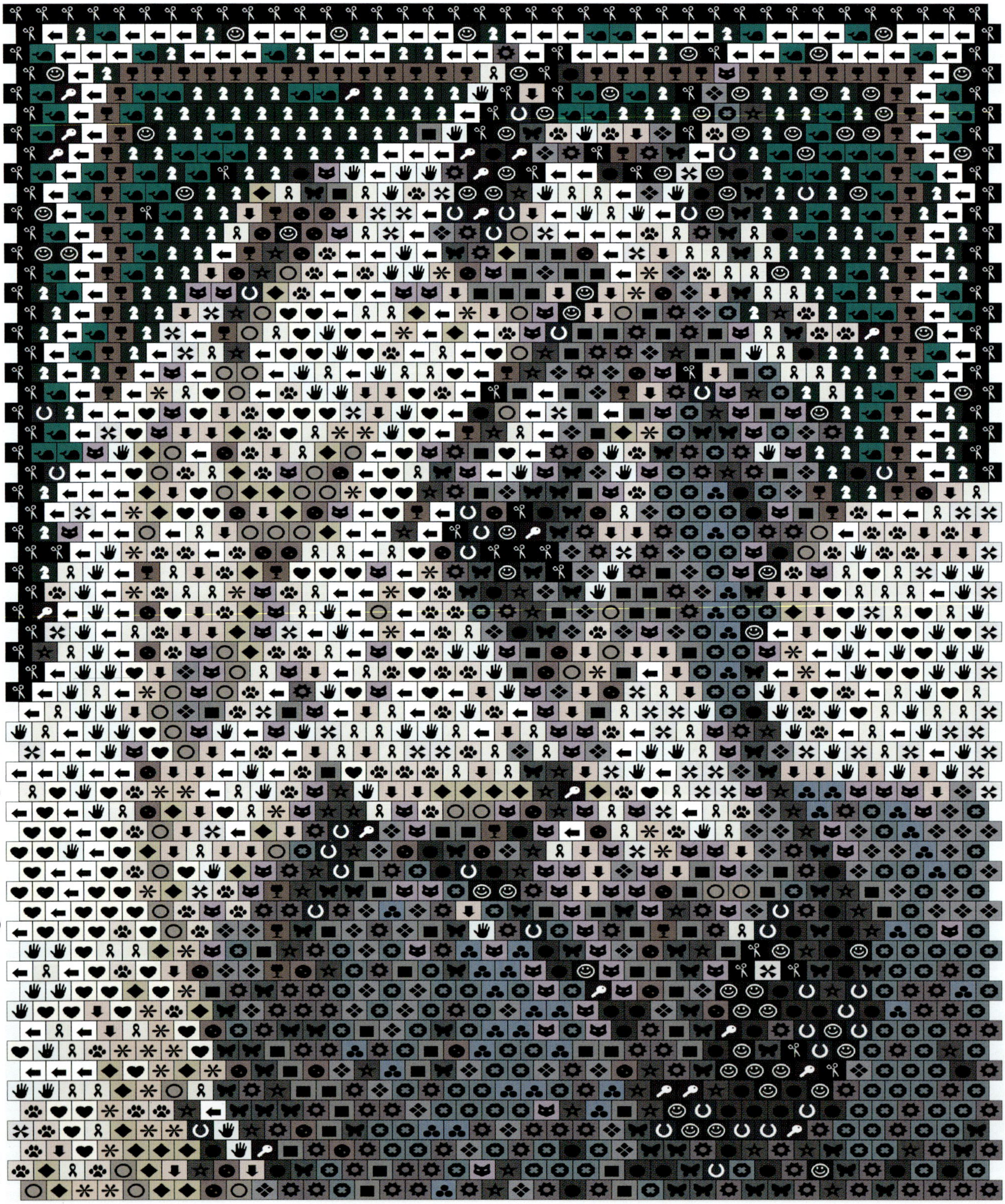

Begin Here - work Peyote Stitch beginning with this row. Work from left to right across the pattern.

For straps and embellishments, gather your own collection of beads, natural stones and crystals. Plan a design that makes the bag uniquely yours. Note: The bead quantities given do not include fringe and strap.

#352 -	Matte Opaque Cream - 102 beads
#211 -	Opaque Alabaster - 43 beads
#242 -	Transparent Pearl Grey - 49 beads
#66 -	Lined Rainbow Crystal White - 87 beads
#708 -	Transparent Grey - 86 beads
#123 -	Transparent Lustre Olive Grey - 80 beads
#351 -	Matte Opaque White - 233 beads
#35 -	Galvanized Silver - 47 beads
#52 -	Lined Rainbow Crystal Ivory - 46 beads
#38 -	Opaque Metallic Palladium Plated - 77 beads
#110 -	Transparent Rainbow Ice Blue - 37 beads
#220 -	Opal White - 54 beads
#301 -	Matte Opaque Blue Grey - 37 beads
#306 -	Matte Opaque Gunmetal - 68 beads
#307 -	Matte Opaque Grey - 60 beads
#741 -	Matte Transparent Crystal - 107 beads
#871 -	Matte Opaque Rainbow Jet - 55 beads
#252 -	Transparent Pearl Grey - 96 beads
#882 -	Matte Rainbow Opaque Grey - 126 beads
#80 -	Lined Rainbow Crystal Lavender - 107 beads
#179 -	Transparent Rainbow Black Diamond - 131 beads
#200 -	Opaque Chalk White - 111 beads
#231 -	Lined Lustre Crystal White - 90 beads
#325 -	Matte Metallic Iris Blue - 20 beads
#310 -	Matte Opaque Black - 123 beads
#858 -	Matte Rainbow Transparent Kelly - 76 beads
#275 -	Lined Opaque Green Teal - 132 beads

The Bear Facts

Silver Bear Paw from Two Pony Trading Post, 147 Royal Rd., Wichita, KS 67207, 316-686-8147
Ceramic Bear Claws from Bally Bead Company, 2304 Ridge Rd., Rockwall, TX 75087, 972-771-4515

'The Bear Facts' is the perfect bag to accent with lots of natural stones, silver, turquoise and other rustic looking materials to give it that outdoors look. I used some porcelain bear claws, little bits of silver, picture jasper and turquoise and carried the color scheme up into the necklace and down into the fringe. Change the colors in the border to give it a whole new look.

Stitch: Peyote or Brick   Size: Approximately $2^1/_2$" x 3"   Beads Used: Delica

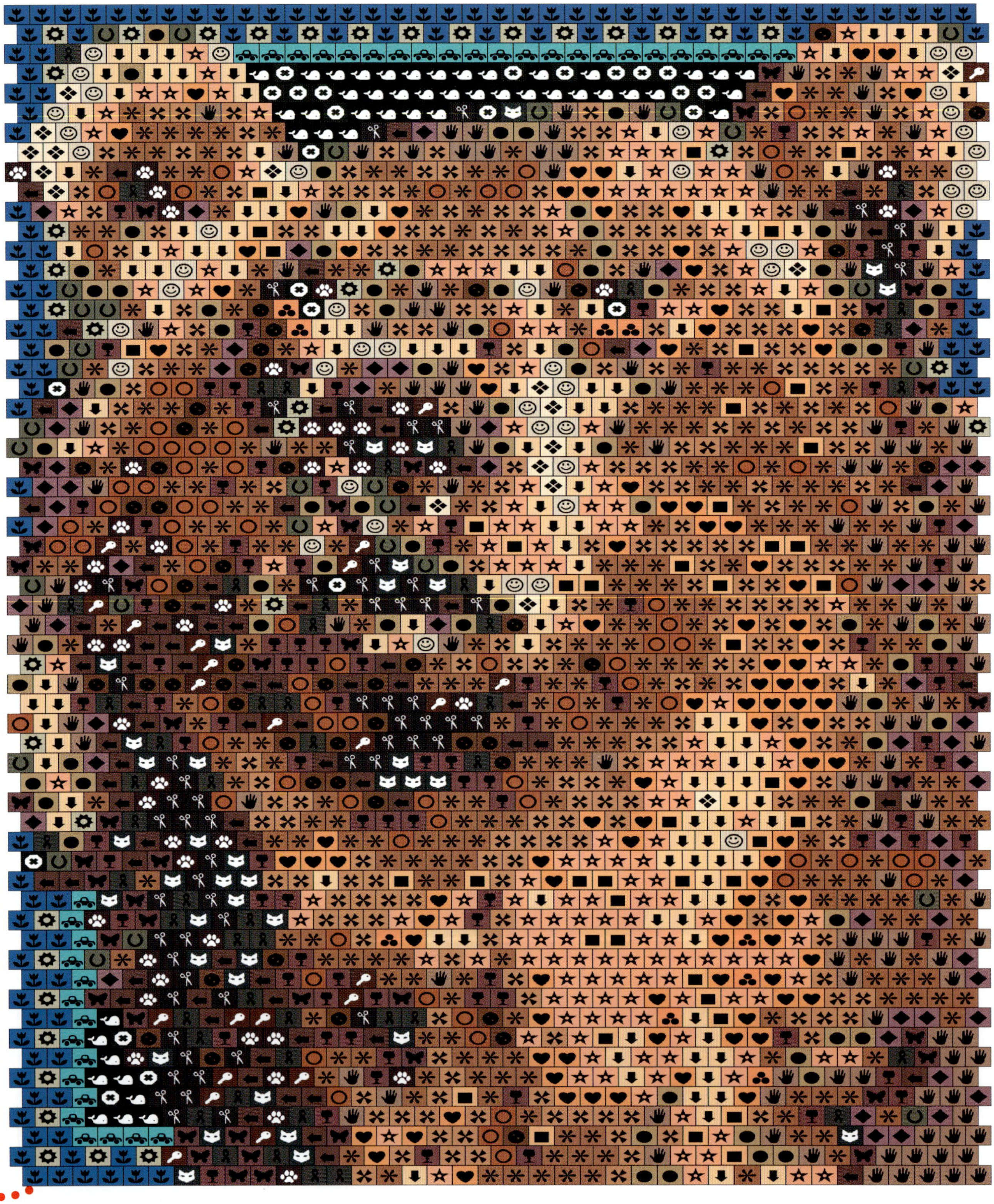

Begin Here - work Peyote Stitch beginning with this row. Work from left to right across the pattern.

For straps and embellishments, gather your own collection of beads, natural stones and crystals. Plan a design that makes the bag uniquely yours. Note: The bead quantities given do not include fringe and strap.

- **#54** - Lined Rainbow Topaz Rose - 103 beads
- **#69** - Lined Rainbow Crystal Tan - 337 beads
- **#102** - Metallic Lustre Rose Gold - 86 beads
- **#205** - Opaque Pearl Beige - 133 beads
- **#208** - Opaque Tan - 45 beads
- **#380** - Matte Metallic Lustre Green Pink - 97 beads
- **#772** - Dyed Matte Transparent Mauve - 79 beads
- **#853** - Matte Rainbow Transparent Dark Topaz - 50 beads
- **#857** - Matte Rainbow Transparent Light Amethyst - 60 beads
- **#884** - Matte Opaque Rainbow Brown - 43 beads
- **#1363** - Dyed Opaque Peach - 9 beads
- **#230** - Lined Opalescent Crystal 24kt Gold - 246 beads
- **#321** - Matte Metallic Silver - 30 beads
- **#762** - Matte Opaque Cream - 47 beads
- **#852** - Matte Rainbow Transparent Light Topaz - 185 beads
- **#256** - Lined Opaque Crystal Taupe - 146 beads
- **#411** - Galvanized Metallic Gold - 81 beads
- **#353** - Matte Opaque Dark Cream - 17 beads
- **#52** - Lined Rainbow Crystal Ivory - 39 beads
- **#301** - Matte Opaque Blue Grey - 38 beads
- **#306** - Matte Opaque Gunmetal - 24 beads
- **#871** - Matte Opaque Rainbow Jet - 50 beads
- **#323** - Matte Metallic Iris Purple - 45 beads
- **#287** - Lined Rainbow Light Topaz Lavender - 24 beads
- **#325** - Matte Metallic Iris Blue - 62 beads
- **#310** - Matte Opaque Black - 47 beads
- **#217** - Opaque Light Aqua - 38 beads
- **#432** - Galvanized Metallic Blue grass - 119 beads

Foxy

This cute little pattern works up quickly and can be accented by everything from glass to crystals. I used some tiny wood beads, glass and a lovely piece of lampwork glass.

Lampwork Accent Bead by Bette Corneliuson, 406-825-7386, chetandbette@blackfoot.net
Side Accents by Felice Osband, 585-288-0130

Stitch: Peyote or Brick | Size: Approximately 2 1/2" x 3" | Beads Used: Delica

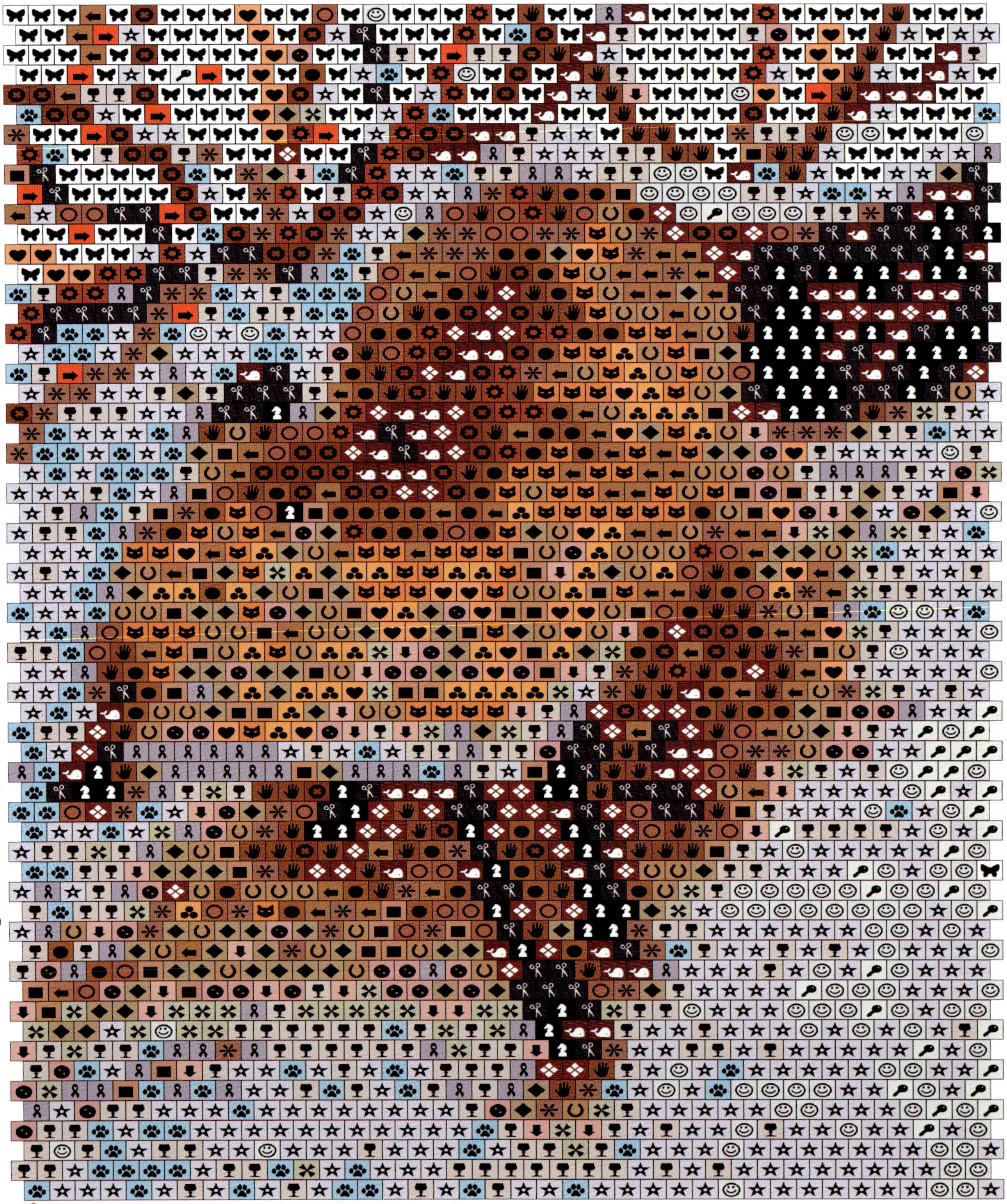

Begin Here - work Peyote Stitch beginning with this row. Work from left to right across the pattern.

For straps and embellishments, gather your own collection of beads, natural stones and crystals. Plan a design that makes the bag uniquely yours. Note: The bead quantities given do not include fringe and strap.

- #54 - Lined Rainbow Topaz Rose - 39 beads
- #69 - Lined Rainbow Crystal Tan - 75 beads
- #102 - Metallic Lustre Rose Gold - 47 beads
- #417 - Galvanized Metallic Pale Lilac - 35 beads
- #230 - Lined Opalescent Crystal 24kt Gold - 54 beads
- #66 Lined Rainbow Crystal White - 192 beads
- #100 - Transparent Rainbow Light Topaz - 68 beads
- #234 - Lined Lustre Crystal Light Pink - 48 beads
- #411 - Galvanized Gold - 91 beads
- #351 - Matte Opaque White - 164 beads
- #702 - Transparent Light Topaz - 39 beads
- #52 - Lined Rainbow Crystal Ivory - 49 beads
- #907 - Lined Sparkle Crystal Light Bronze - 84 beads
- #220 - Opal White - 104 beads
- #357 - Matte Light Grey - 348 beads
- #221 - Opaque Metallic Light Bronze - 88 beads
- #34 - Opaque Metallic Light Gold - 65 beads
- #121 - Transparent Lustre Dark Topaz - 58 beads
- #122 - Light Brown Iris - 39 beads
- #272 - Lined Opaque Topaz Yellow - 70 beads
- #794 - Sienna Brown - 64 beads
- #80 - Lined Rainbow Crystal Lavender - 72 beads
- #83 - Lined Rainbow Crystal Light Aqua - 109 beads
- #200 - Chalk White - 31 beads
- #325 - Matte Metallic Iris Blue - 101 beads
- #23 - Metallic Iris Light Bronze - 71 beads
- #310 - Matte Opaque Black - 62 beads
- #295 - Lined Opaque Ruby Red - 3 beads

Winter's Teeth

A white wolf against a snowy white background... stay with the colors I gave for the border or substitute your own! Accent with stones, crystals or silver. Almost anything will work with this fellow!

Blue Lampwork in Strap by Morebeads, beads@morebeads.com
Sample by Dawn Marvin, Mourning Dove Makings, Wichita, KS, mourndovemakes@hotmail.com

Stitch: Peyote or Brick

Size: Approximately 2 1/2" x 3"

Beads Used: Delica

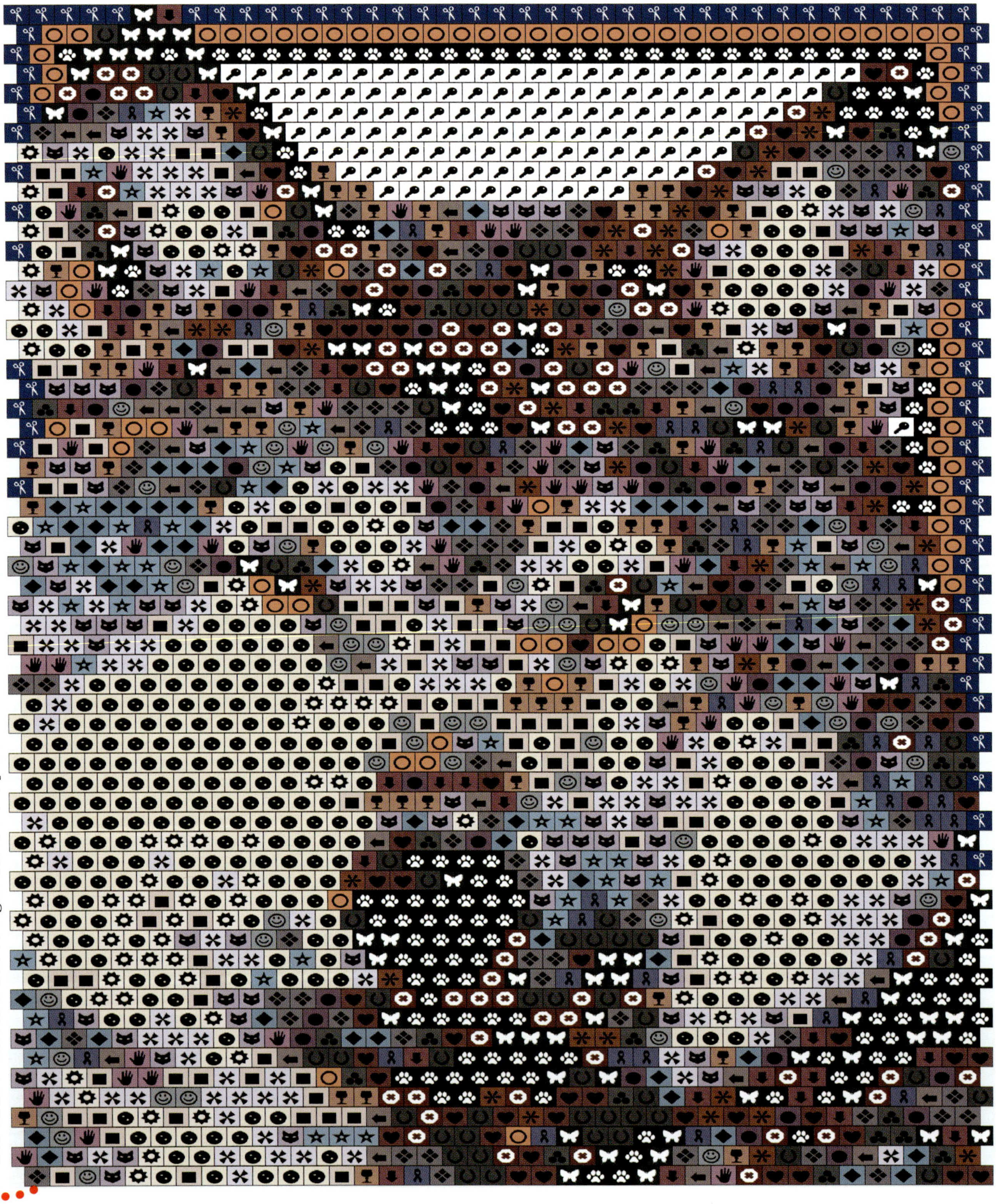

Begin Here - work Peyote Stitch beginning with this row. Work from left to right across the pattern.

For straps and embellishments, gather your own collection of beads, natural stones and crystals. Plan a design that makes the bag uniquely yours. Note: The bead quantities given do not include fringe and strap.

#772 - Dyed Matte Transparent Mauve - 83 beads

#853 - Matte Rainbow Transparent Dark Topaz - 45 beads

#230 - Lined Opalescent Crystal 24kt Gold - 81 beads

#884 - Matte Opaque Rainbow Brown - 48 beads

#66 - Lined Rainbow Crystal White- 127 beads

#256 - Lined Opaque Crystal Taupe - 87 beads

#35 - Galvanized Silver - 56 beads

#851 - Matte Rainbow Transparent Crystal - 331 beads

#110 - Transparent Rainbow Ice Blue - 66 beads

#306 - Mate Opaque Gunmetal - 83 beads

#307 - Matte Opaque Grey - 35 beads

#357 - Matte Light Grey - 44 beads

#871 - Matte Opaque Rainbow Jet - 75 beads

#252 - Transparent Pearl Grey - 63 beads

#257 - Lined Transparent Crystal Light Sapphire - 50 beads

#379 - Matte Metallic Lavender - 54 beads

#765 - Matte Transparent Lilac - 58 beads

#882 - Matte Rainbow Opaque Grey - 112 beads

#201 - Opaque Pearl White - 83 beads

#80 - Lined Rainbow Crystal Lavender - 113 beads

#287 - Lined Rainbow Light Topaz Lavender - 78 beads

#111 - Transparent Rainbow Black Diamond - 50 beads

#310 - Matte Black - 141 beads

#351 - Matte White - 127 beads

#285 - Lined Opaque Light Aqua Royal Blue - 90 beads

- #37 - Lined Metallic Crystal Copper - 14 beads
- #54 - Lined Rainbow Topaz Rose - 71 beads
- #69 - Lined Rainbow Crystal Tan - 44 beads
- #102 - Metallic Lustre Rose Gold - 172 beads
- #208 - Opaque Tan - 41 beads
- #420 - Galvanized Metallic Dark Pink - 25 beads
- #857 - Matte Rainbow Transparent Light Amethyst - 44 beads
- #901 - Lined Sparkle Crystal Topaz - 100 beads
- #146 - Silver Lined Light Amethyst - 233 beads
- #230 - Lined Opalescent Crystal 24kt Gold - 9 beads
- #234 - Lined Lustre Crystal Light Pink - 65 beads
- #411 - Galvanized Gold - 5 beads
- #912 - Lined Sparkle Topaz Light Amethyst - 81 beads
- #301 - Matte Opaque Blue Grey - 45 beads
- #306 - Matte Opaque Gunmetal - 36 beads
- #465 - Galvanized Metallic Midnight Blue - 5 beads
- #871 - Matte Opaque Rainbow Jet - 48 beads
- #117 - Metallic Lustre Light Sapphire Red - 9 beads
- #158 - Opaque Rainbow Lilac - 34 beads
- #173 - Transparent Rainbow Light Amethyst - 45 beads
- #356 - Matte Opaque Lavender - 48 beads
- #379 - Matte Metallic Lavender - 42 beads
- #454 - Galvanized Metallic Light Grape - 53 beads
- #865 - Matte Rainbow Transparent Smoke Topaz - 70 beads
- #882 - Matte Rainbow Opaque Grey - 21 beads
- #323 - Matte Metallic Iris Purple - 47 beads
- #22L - Opaque Metallic Light Bronze - 146 beads
- #26 - Metallic Dark Steel - 49 beads
- #1 - Hematite - 499 beads
- #179 - Transparent Rainbow Black Diamond - 47 beads
- #325 - Matte Metallic Iris Blue - 122 beads

Sundown

This is a very colorful design and can lend itself to many different methods of finishing. I chose a lovely, handmade lampwork bead which picked up the colors in the sunset; however, you could just as easily use glass, stone or other accents on your spirit bag!

Lampwork Accent Bead by Bette Corneliuson,
6905 Slide Rock Dr., Clinton, MT 59825, 406-825-7386
chetandbette@blackfoot.net

Stitch: Peyote or Brick

Size: Approximately 2 1/2" x 3"

Beads Used: Delica

Begin Here - work Peyote Stitch beginning with this row. Work from left to right across the pattern.

For straps and embellishments, gather your own collection of beads, natural stones and crystals. Plan a design that makes the bag uniquely yours. Note: The bead quantities given do not include fringe and strap.

Desert Dusk

This pattern depicting a desert at the moment the sun starts to dip below the mountains is colorful and bright! I chose a piece of dichroic glass to accent mine but you could use Czech glass, crystals or stones for accents on yours! There are so many colors here to pull out for your accents. Have fun with it!

Dichroic Lampwork Accent Bead by
Linda Greene, Copper Moon Cat, 703-383-9083
coppery164@cs.com
Sample by Roberta Dildine, B&D Designs
bddildine@designsbydeb.com

Stitch: Peyote or Brick

Size: Approximately $2^1/_2$" x 3"

Beads Used: Delica

Begin Here - work Peyote Stitch beginning with this row. Work from left to right across the pattern.

For straps and embellishments, gather your own collection of beads, natural stones and crystals. Plan a design that makes the bag uniquely yours. Note: The bead quantities given do not include fringe and strap.

- #37 - Lined Metallic Crystal Copper - 9 beads
- #54 - Lined Rainbow Topaz Rose - 43 beads
- #208 - Opaque Tan - 25 beads
- #417 - Galvanized Metallic Pale Lilac - 48 beads
- #857 - Matte Rainbow Transparent Light Amethyst - 23 beads
- #863 - Matte Rainbow Transparent Grey - 47 beads
- #230 - Lined Opalescent Crystal 24kt Gold - 51 beads
- #234 - Lined Lustre Crystal Light Pink - 148 beads
- #462 - Galvanized Metallic Dark Grey Mauve - 36 beads
- #852 - Matte Rainbow Transparent Light Topaz - 30 beads
- #411 - Galvanized Gold - 66 beads
- #107 - Transparent Grey Iris - 47 beads
- #301 - Matte Opaque Blue Grey - 99 beads
- #132 - Opaque Dark Grey Rainbow - 119 beads
- #307 - Matte Opaque Grey - 45 beads
- #376 - Matte Metallic Denim Blue - 46 beads
- #871 - Matte Opaque Rainbow Jet - 121 beads
- #881 - Matte Rainbow Opaque Periwinkle - 211 beads
- #117 - Metallic Lustre Light Sapphire Red - 8 beads
- #158 - Opaque Rainbow Lilac - 16 beads
- #252 - Transparent Pearl Grey - 103 beads
- #257 - Lined Transparent Crystal Light Sapphire - 116 beads
- #758 - Matte Opaque Lilac - 156 beads
- #80 - Lined Rainbow Crystal Lavender - 114 beads
- #325 - Matte Metallic Iris Blue - 132 beads
- #111 - Transparent Rainbow Black Diamond - 45 beads
- #1 - Hematite - 376 beads

Soaring Eagle

Due to the shape of this design, it is best to use brick stitch rather than peyote. Find an area which has the widest solid row of beads, probably in the shoulder area, and start your base row at that point. Work down from there, through the body. When finished, work up through the wings.

The beader who made the sample shown, made tabs at the top of each wing tip and then ran her strands of beads up from that. You could also make a solid strip of beadwork for the necklace.

Stitch: Brick
Size: Approximately 7$\frac{1}{2}$" x 7$\frac{1}{2}$"
Beads Used: Delica

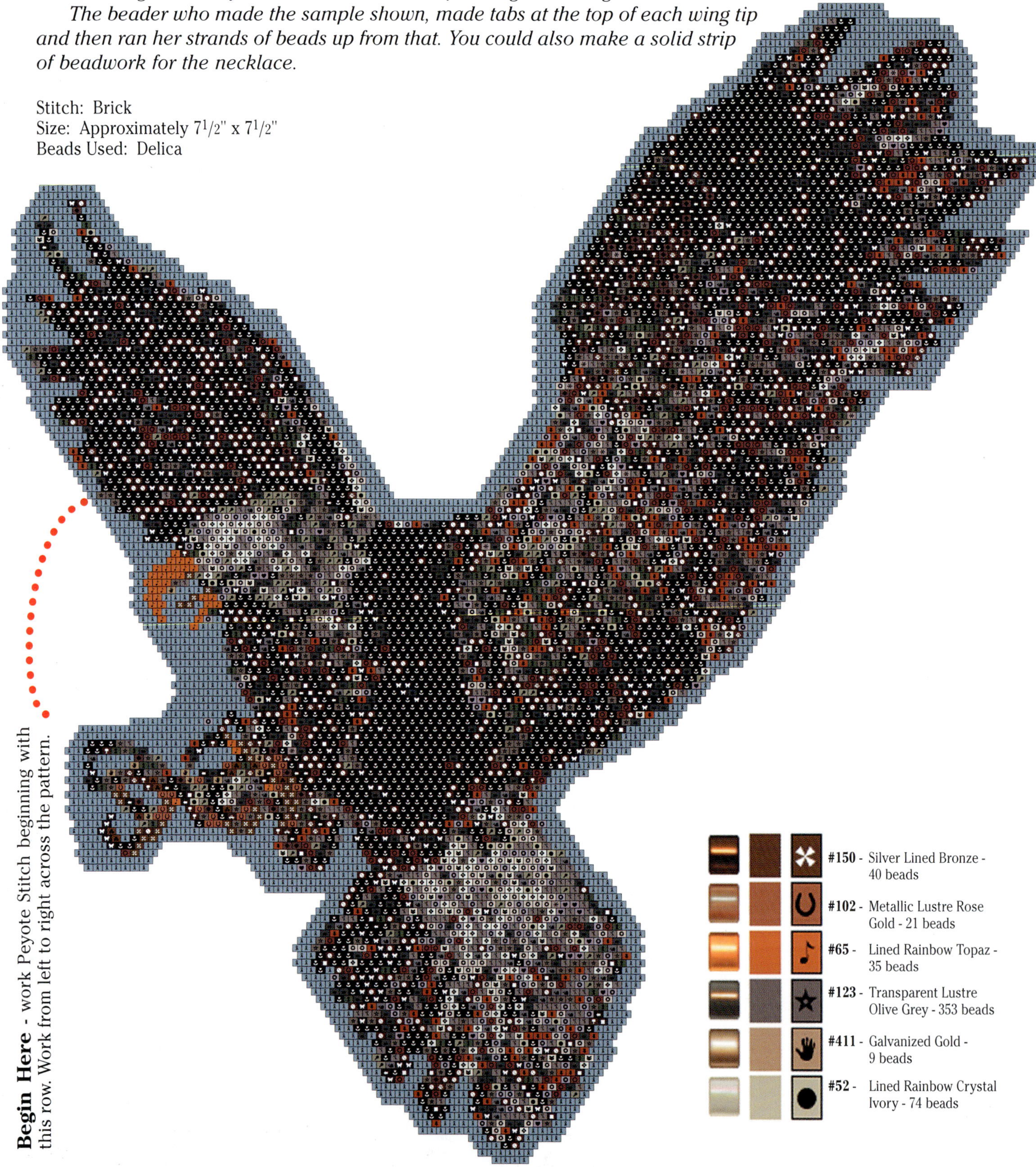

Begin Here - work Peyote Stitch beginning with this row. Work from left to right across the pattern.

- **#150** - Silver Lined Bronze - 40 beads
- **#102** - Metallic Lustre Rose Gold - 21 beads
- **#65** - Lined Rainbow Topaz - 35 beads
- **#123** - Transparent Lustre Olive Grey - 353 beads
- **#411** - Galvanized Gold - 9 beads
- **#52** - Lined Rainbow Crystal Ivory - 74 beads

For straps and embellishments, gather your own collection of beads, natural stones and crystals. Plan a design that makes the bag uniquely yours. Note: The bead quantities given do not include fringe and strap.

#758 - Matte Opaque Lilac - 47 beads

#863 - Matte Rainbow Transparent Grey - 13 beads

#865 - Matte Rainbow Transparent Smoke Topaz - 347 beads

#122 - Light Brown Iris - 226 beads

#323 - Matte Metallic Iris Purple - 154 beads

#312 - Matte Metallic Copper - 97 beads

#769 - Matte Transparent Root Beer - 106 beads

#87 - Lined Rainbow Topaz - 498 beads

#772 - Dyed Matte Transparent Mauve - 60 beads

#325 - Matte Metallic Iris Blue - 292 beads

#322 - Matte Metallic Gold - 10 beads

#200 - Chalk White - 158 beads

#66 - Lined Rainbow Crystal White - 221 beads

#851 - Matte Rainbow Transparent Crystal - 68 beads

#80 - Lined Rainbow Crystal Lavender - 182 beads

#257 - Lined Transparent Crystal Light Sapphire - 1559 beads

#287 - Lined Rainbow Light Topaz Lavender - 66 beads

#336 - Matte Metallic Palladium Plated - 136 beads

#35 - Galvanized Silver - 344 beads

#882 - Matte Rainbow Opaque Grey - 140 beads

#251 - Metallic Lustre Grey - 123 beads

#871 - Matte Opaque Rainbow Jet - 480 beads

#310 - Matte Black - 2155 beads

#734 - Opaque Chocolate Brown - 5 beads

Large Lampwork on Strap by Sandra Seaman, sandree@appleisp.net or http://www.onebead.com

Small Lampwork by S&L Designs yagerls@navix.net.

Sample by Suzanne Siegel P.O. Box 2152 Kalispell, MT 59903, ssiegel@cyberport.net

Captured Dreams

This is a unique design in that it provides the opportunity to add little stones and crystals to the dream catcher when you finish! The string work doesn't have to be perfect, just think of a spider's web while you are working it and have fun putting your own good luck stones into the design!

Stitch: Peyote or Brick | Size: Approximately 2 1/2" x 3" | Beads Used: Delica

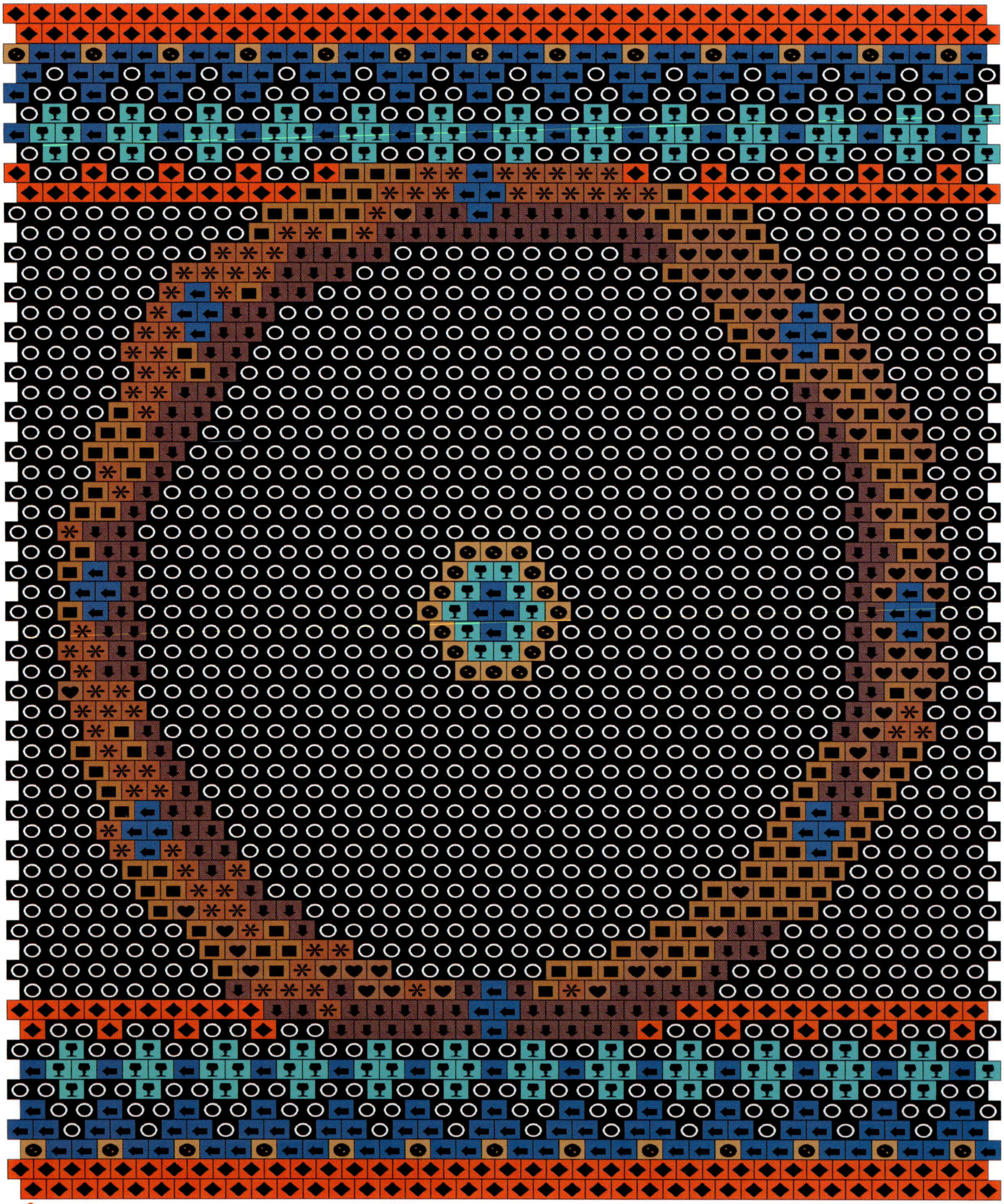

Begin Here - work Peyote Stitch beginning with this row. Work from left to right across the pattern.

For straps and embellishments, gather your own collection of beads, natural stones and crystals. Plan a design that makes the bag uniquely yours. Note: The bead quantities given do not include fringe and strap.

#69 - Lined Rainbow Crystal Tan - 69 beads

#102 - Metallic Lustre Rose Gold - 79 beads

#310 - Matte Opaque Black - 1332 beads

#884 - Matte Opaque Rainbow Brown - 134 beads

#100 - Transparent Rainbow Light Topaz - 109 beads

#217 - Opaque Light Aqua - 110 beads

#432 - Galvanized Metallic Blue grass - 189 beads

#410 - Galvanized Bright Gold - 42 beads

#757 - Matte Opaque Light Red - 216 beads

Gold Feather Accents from Bally Bead Company, 2304 Ridge Rd., Rockwall, TX 75087, www.ballybead.com

This is definitely an easy pattern to finish! While it looks complex, I've added a few markers that will help you place your string work on the finished beading.

Insert a piece of stiff cardboard into the finished bag to hold it flat. Anchor your thread in the beadwork and come out through one of the Blue beads in the ring. It makes no difference where you start, any place is fine!

NOTE: The Blue beads are shaped like diamonds. Think of these as your bases. The one where you began is base 1, the next base 2 and so on around the circle, 8 in all. Going from base 1, find the inside most bead on base 2 (the diamond bead facing the center of the circle) and run your needle through that bead so that it goes back toward base 1. Pull the thread snug, but not tight. Go to base 3 and run the needle through the inside bead of that diamond toward base 2, snug the thread. Repeat around the circle until you are back at base 1 and run the thread back through the inner bead toward base 8. When you exit, you should have a circle of thread around your beadwork. The thread should cross itself at each diamond EXCEPT at the top and bottom diamonds because the beads on these face up and down rather than sideways. Place needle on the thread between base 1 and base 2, run under the thread toward the center of the circle and come up between base 1 and the new thread. Pull snug toward base 2 and it will form a loop around the original circle thread which will help keep it in place. Go to the area between base 2 and base 3 and repeat running your needle under the existing thread toward the center and coming out between the new thread and base 2. Continue around in this fashion and work to center. Add crystals and stones as you work. Tie off on the nearest thread and add a drop of clear nail polish to secure.

Four Directions Rug

These lovely rug inspired designs are the perfect finish for your beaded bags. The patterns can be mixed and matched for use with different front designs.

Stitch: Peyote or Brick   Size: Approximately $2^{1}/_{2}$" x 3"   Beads Used: Delica

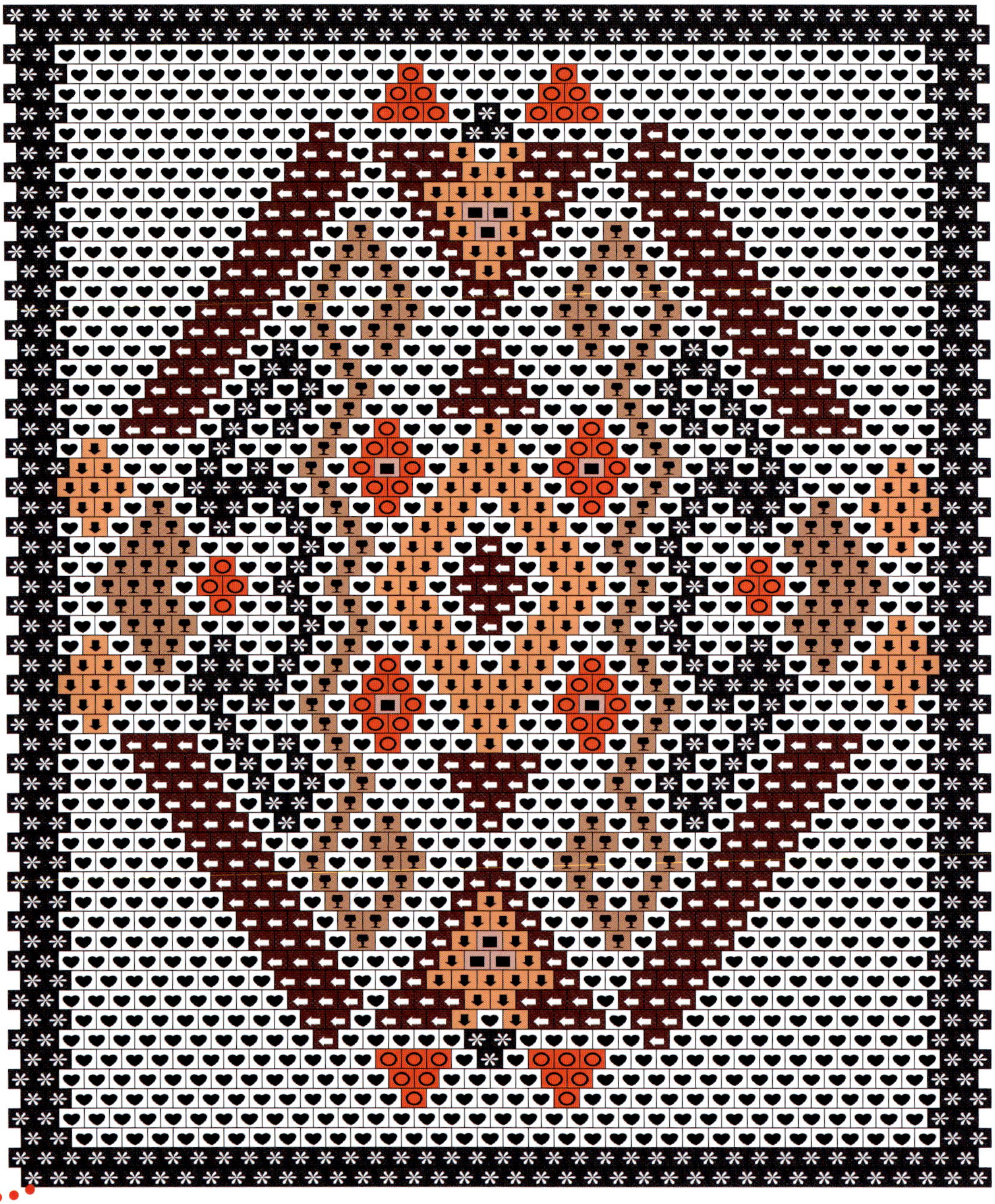

Begin Here - work Peyote Stitch beginning with this row. Work from left to right across the pattern.

Foxy Back

Contemplation Back

Sundown Back

Desert Dusk Back

For straps and embellishments, gather your own collection of beads, natural stones and crystals. Plan a design that makes the bag uniquely yours. Note: The bead quantities given do not include fringe and strap.

Foxy Back

- **#351** - Matte Opaque White - 1199 beads
- **#325** - Matte Metallic Iris Blue - 476 beads
- **#295** - Lined Opaque Ruby Red - 64 beads
- **#54** - Lined Rainbow Topaz Rose - 124 beads
- **#417** - Galvanized Metallic Pale Lilac - 10 beads
- **#230** - Lined Opalescent Crystal 24kt Gold - 148 beads
- **#23** - Metallic Iris Light Bronze - 259 beads

Contemplation Back

- **#52** - Lined Rainbow Crystal Ivory - 148 beads
- **#411** - Galvanized Gold - 124 beads
- **#114** - Transparent Lustre Silver Grey - 65 beads
- **#352** - Matte Opaque Light Cream - 1199 beads
- **#205** - Opaque Pearl Beige - 10 beads
- **#865** - Matte Rainbow Transparent Smoke Topaz - 259 beads
- **#325** - Matte Metallic Iris Blue - 475 beads

Sundown Back

- **#234** - Lined Lustre Crystal Pale Pink - 158 beads
- **#117** - Metallic Lustre Topaz Red - 259 beads
- **#1** - Hematite - 476 beads
- **#901** - Lined Sparkle Crystal Topaz - 64 beads
- **#379** - Matte Metallic Lavender - 1199 beads
- **#22L** - Opaque Metallic Light Bronze - 124 beads

Desert Dusk Back

- **#54** - Lined Rainbow Topaz Rose - 148 beads
- **#234** - Lined Lustre Crystal Pale Pink - 10 beads
- **#411** - Galvanized Gold - 124 beads
- **#881** - Matte Rainbow Opaque Periwinkle - 64 bead
- **#3117** -Metallic Lustre Topaz Red - 259 beads
- **#758** - Matte Opaque Lilac - 1199 beads
- **#1** - Hematite - 476 beads

As another option to give Spirit Horse a Green color scheme, use: Heart - **#411**, Star - **#123**, Circle - **#351**, Down Arrow - **#110**, Cube - **#310**, Wine Glass - **#858** and Left Arrow - **#275.**

Winter's Teeth Back

♥	#351 -	Matte Opaque White - 826 beads
✻	#310 -	Matte Opaque Black - 568 beads
🍷	#230 -	Lined Opalescent Crystals 24kt Gold - 262 beads
⁚	#296 -	Lined Transparent Dark Topaz Ruby - 84 beads
←	#285 -	Lined Opaque Light Aqua Royal Blue - 540 beads

Kachina Back

♥	#351 -	Matte Opaque White - 826 beads
✻	#1 -	Hematite - 568 beads
🍷	#460 -	Galvanized Metallic Rose Gold - 262 beads
⁚	#111 -	Transparent Rainbow Black Diamond - 84 beads
←	#117 -	Metallic Lustre Light Sapphire Red - 540 beads

Spirit Horse Back

♥	#351 -	Matte Opaque White - 826 beads
✻	#310 -	Matte Opaque Black - 568 beads
🍷	#123 -	Transparent Lustre Olive Grey - 262 beads
⁚	#110 -	Transparent Rainbow Ice Blue - 84 beads
←	#275 -	Lined Opaque Green Teal - 540 beads

Winter's Teeth or Contemplation Back

Symbol	Bead	Description
✻	#310 -	Matte Opaque Black - 570 beads
🍷	#230 -	Lined Opalescent Crystal 24kt Gold - 264 beads
♥	#883 -	Matte Rainbow Opaque Ivory - 826 beads
⁚	#865 -	Matte Rainbow Transparent Smoke Topaz - 84 beads
←	#111 -	Transparent Rainbow Black Diamond - 536 beads

Indian Rug

Feel free to substitute your own color schemes in place of the ones given here. Just choose the colors you want.

Stitch: Peyote or Brick

Size: Approximately 2 1/2" x 3"

Beads Used: Delica

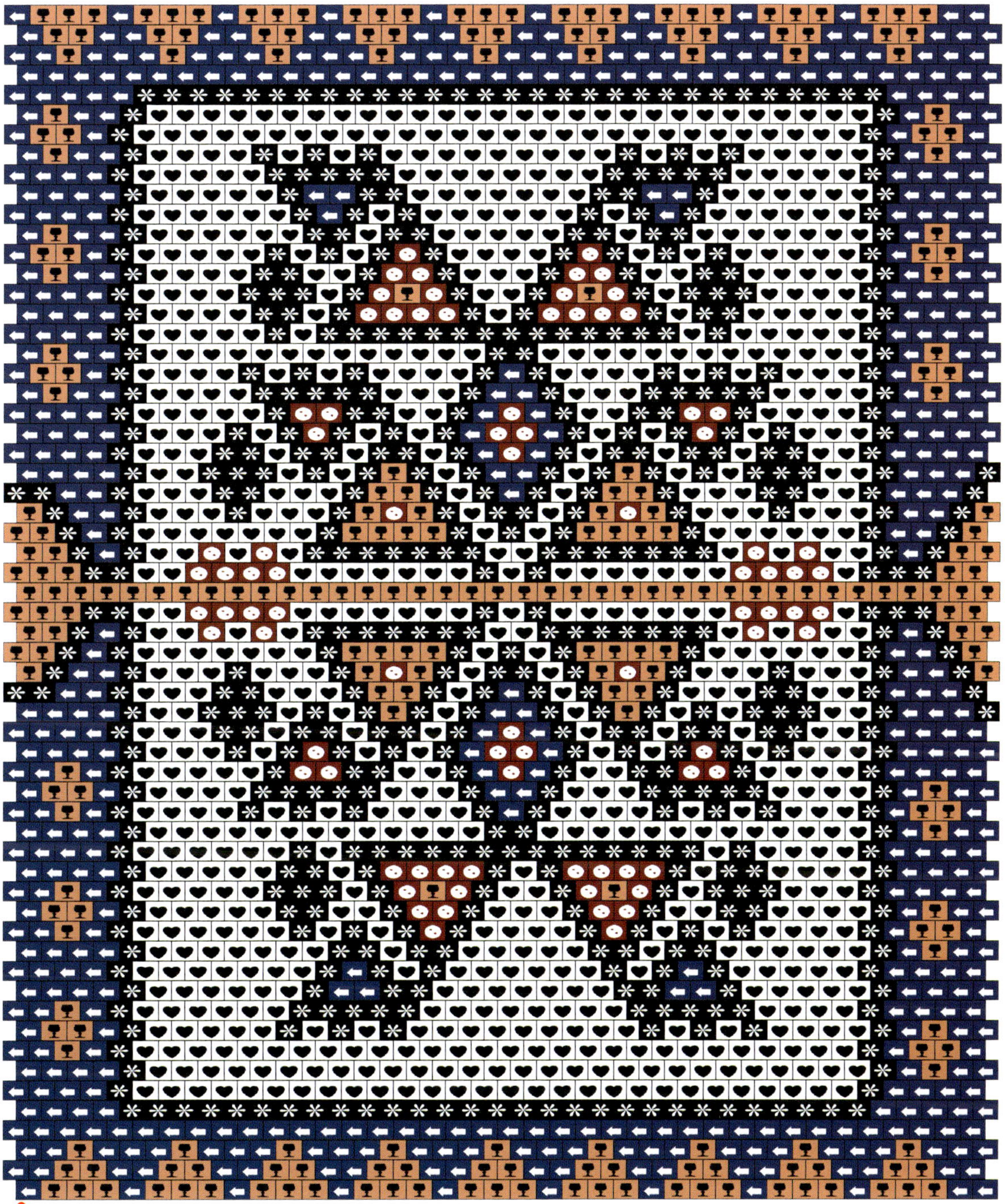

Begin Here - work Peyote Stitch beginning with this row. Work from left to right across the pattern.

Winter's Teeth Back

Kachina Back

Spirit Horse Back

Winter's Teeth or Contemplation Back

For straps and embellishments, gather your own collection of beads, natural stones and crystals. Plan a design that makes the bag uniquely yours. Note: The bead quantities given do not include fringe and strap.

Native Rug

This rug design can take on a variety of looks. Choose vibrant Southwestern colors or use metallics for a subtle richness. Any color combination will be a joy to wear!

Stitch: Peyote or Brick Size: Approximately 2 1/2" x 3" Beads Used: Delica

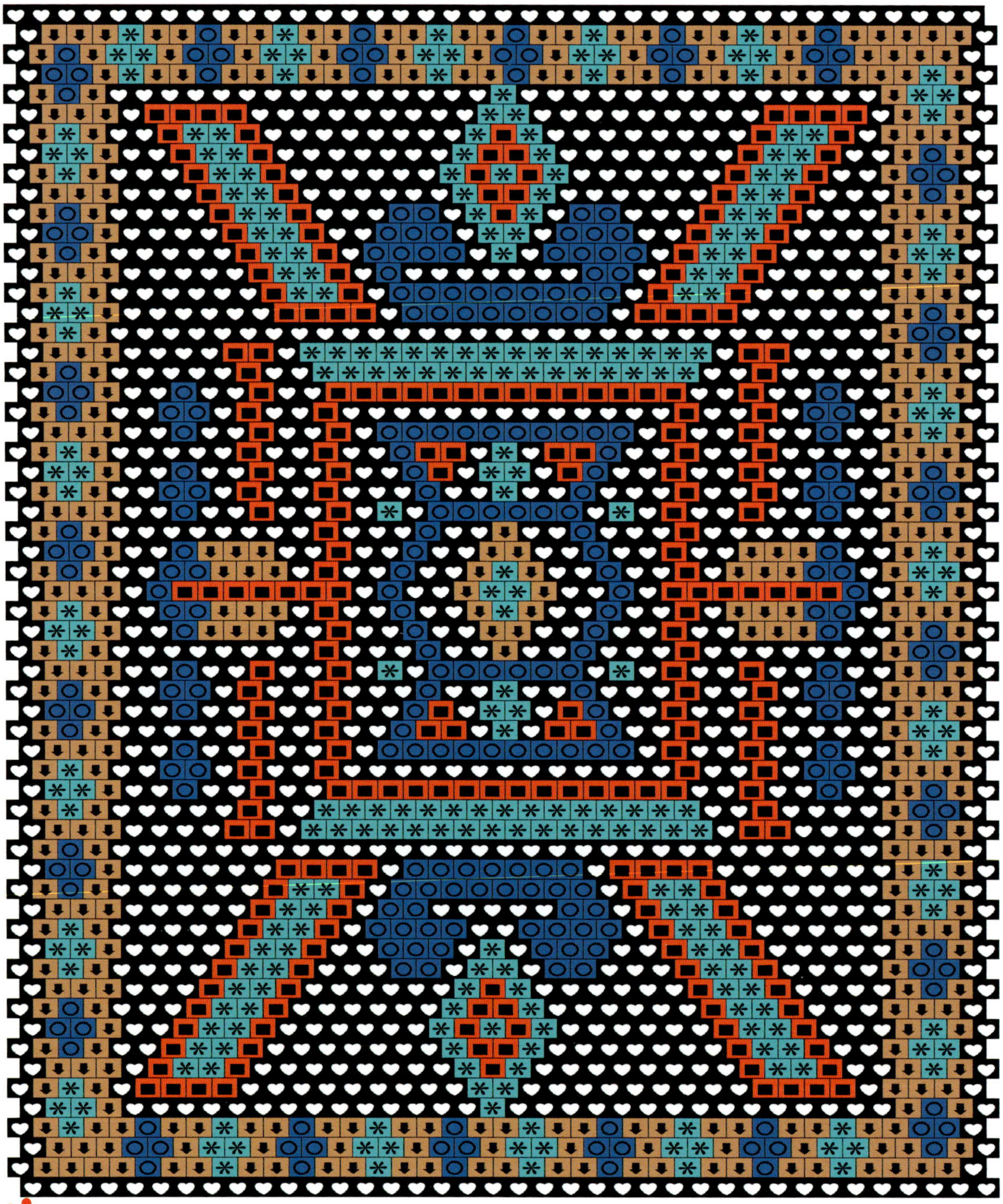

Begin Here - work Peyote Stitch beginning with this row. Work from left to right across the pattern.

The Bear Facts Back

Captured Dreams Back

Kachina, Desert Dusk or Sundown Back

Alpha Wolf

For straps and embellishments, gather your own collection of beads, natural stones and crystals. Plan a design that makes the bag uniquely yours. Note: The bead quantities given do not include fringe and strap.

'The Bear Facts' Back

- **#52** - Lined Rainbow Crystal Ivory - 372 beads
- **#306** - Matte Opaque Gunmetal - 1094 beads
- **#1363** -Dyed Opaque Peach - 254 beads
- **#217** - Opaque Light Aqua - 276 beads
- **#432** - Galvanized Metallic Bluegrass - 284 beads

Captured Dreams Back

- **#310** - Matte Opaque Black - 1095 beads
- **#217** - Opaque Light Aqua - 284 beads
- **#432** - Galvanized Metallic Bluegrass - 275 beads
- **#410** - Galvanized Bright Gold - 372 beads
- **#757** - Matte Opaque Light Red - 254 beads

Kachina, Desert Dusk or Sundown Back

- **#310** - Matte Opaque Black - 1095 beads
- **#146** - Sliver Lined Light Amethyst - 254 beads
- **#234** - Lined Lustre Crystal Light Pink - 275 beads
- **#117** - Metallic Lustre Light Sapphire Red - 284 beads
- **#460** - Galvanized Metallic Rose Gold - 372 beads

Alpha Wolf

- **#35** - Galvanized Silver - 372 beads
- **#205** - Opaque Pearl Beige - 254 beads
- **#306** - Matte Opaque Gunmetal - 1095 beads
- **#111** - Transparent Rainbow Black Diamond - 275 beads
- **#37** - Lined Metallic Crystal Copper - 284 beads

Kachina

This is a very colorful design with lots of lavenders, blues and pinks! I accented mine with freshwater pearls in various colors, but you could also use glass, crystals and stones. Amethyst would make an excellent accent!

Sterling Kokopelli Earrings with Opal Insets,
John Monteith, PO Box 94448, Phoenix AZ 85070
dialilmfg@aol.com

Stitch: Peyote or Brick

Size: Approximately $2^1/_2$" x 3"

Beads: Delica

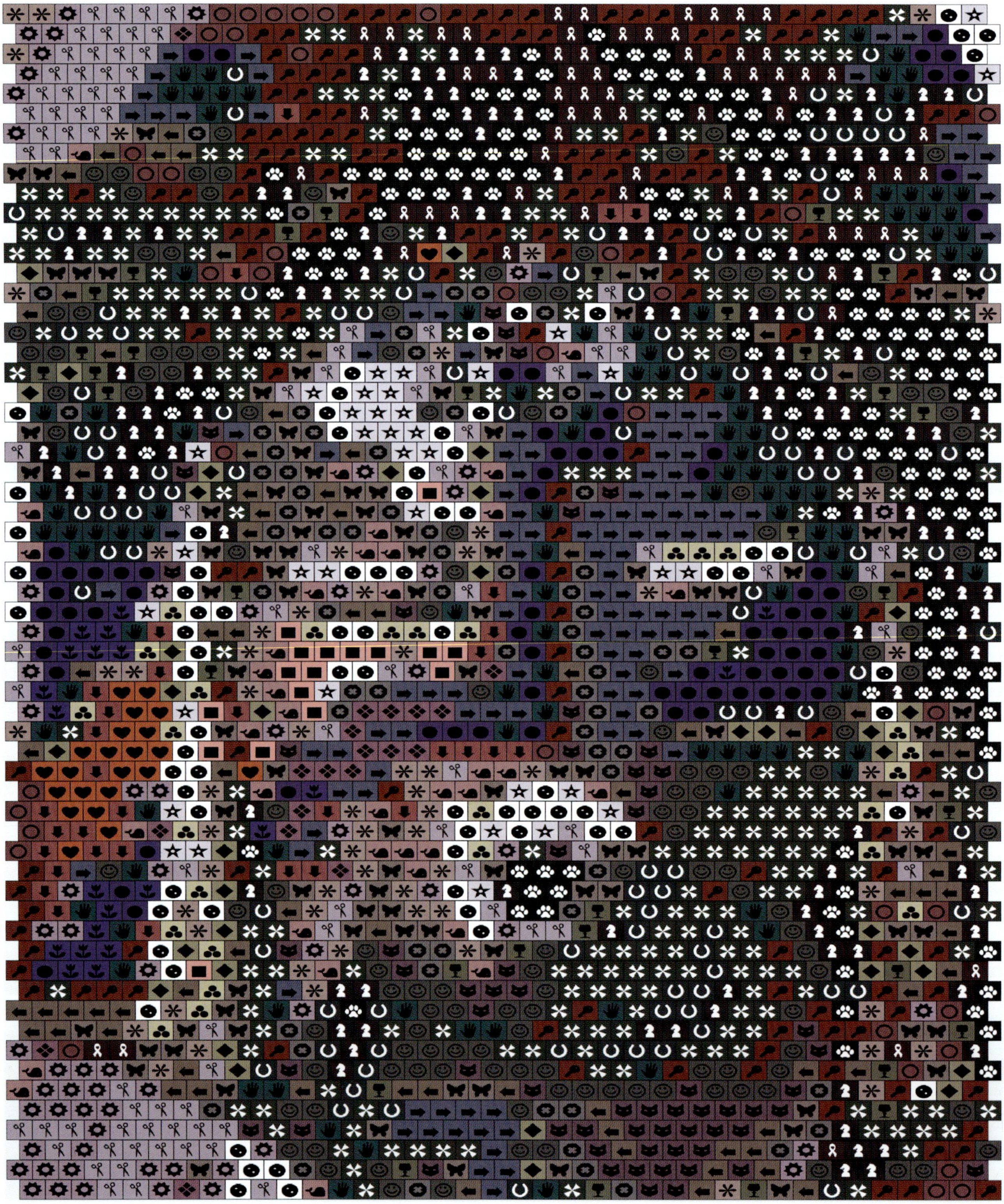

Begin Here - work Peyote Stitch beginning with this row. Work from left to right across the pattern.

For straps and embellishments, gather your own collection of beads, natural stones and crystals. Plan a design that makes the bag uniquely yours. Note: The bead quantities given do not include fringe and strap.

#102 - Metallic Lustre Rose Gold - 23 beads

#863 - Matte Rainbow Transparent Grey - 63 beads

#884 - Matte Opaque Rainbow Brown - 39 beads

#146 - Silver Lined Light Amethyst - 33 beads

#234 - Lined Lustre Crystal Light Pink - 17 beads

#321 - Matte Metallic Silver - 35 beads

#123 - Transparent Lustre Olive Grey - 82 beads

#351 - Matte White - 78 beads

#336 - Matte Metallic Palladium Plated - 36 beads

#35 - Galvanized Silver - 97 beads

#52 - Lined Rainbow Crystal Ivory - 27 beads

#132 - Opaque Dark Grey Rainbow - 256 beads

#301 - Matte Opaque Blue Grey - 111 beads

#307 - Matte Opaque Grey - 140 beads

#357 - Matte Light Grey - 37 beads

#451 - Galvanized Metallic Denim Blue - 110 beads

#117 - Metallic Lustre Light Sapphire Red - 75 beads

#158 - Opaque Rainbow Lilac - 19 beads

#758 - Matte Opaque Lilac - 68 beads

#765 - Matte Transparent Lilac - 62 beads

#882 - Matte Rainbow Opaque Grey - 69 beads

#323 - Matte Metallic Iris Purple - 67 beads

#1 - Hematite - 163 beads

#460 - Galvanized Metallic Rose Gold - 155 beads

#80 - Lined Rainbow Crystal Lavender - 94 beads

#875 - Matte Rainbow Opaque Lilac - 37 beads

#325 - Matte Metallic Iris Blue - 140 beads

#111 - Transparent Rainbow Black Diamond - 126 beads

#880 - Matte Rainbow Opaque Royal Blue - 21 beads

- #54 - Lined Rainbow Topaz Rose - 83 beads
- #69 - Lined Rainbow Crystal Tan - 79 beads
- #102 - Metallic Lustre Rose Gold - 163 beads
- #205 - Opaque Pearl Beige - 49 beads
- #208 - Opaque Tan - 99 beads
- #380 - Matte Metallic Lustre Green Pink - 40 beads
- #772 - Dyed Matte Transparent Mauve - 49 beads
- #853 - Matte Rainbow Transparent Dark Topaz - 54 beads
- #857 - Matte Rainbow Transparent Lt Amethyst - 448 beads
- #863 - Matte Rainbow Transparent Grey - 1278 beads
- #884 - Matte Opaque Rainbow Brown - 43 beads
- #230 - Lined Opalescent Crystal 24 kt Gold - 549 beads
- #242 - Transparent Pearl Grey - 83 beads
- #100 - Transparent Rainbow Light Topaz - 88 beads
- #702 - Transparent Light Topaz - 60 beads
- #256 - Lined Opaque Crystal Taupe - 55 beads
- #131 - Pink Lustre Moss Green - 41 beads
- #52 - Lined Rainbow Crystal Ivory - 40 beads
- #306 - Matte Opaque Gunmetal - 1159 beads
- #307 - Matte Opaque Grey - 142 beads
- #861 - Matte Rainbow Transparent Sky Blue - 145 beads
- #871 - Matte Opaque Rainbow Jet - 117 beads
- #865 Matte Rainbow Transparent Smoke Topaz - 817 beads
- #882 - Matte Rainbow Opaque Grey - 87 beads
- #323 - Matte Metallic Iris Purple - 102 beads
- #202 - Pearl Rainbow White - 307 beads
- #734 - Opaque Chocolate Brown - 35 beads
- #287 - Lined Rainbow Light Topaz Lavender - 46 beads
- #773 - Dyed Matte Transparent Cherry - 65 beads
- #325 - Matte Metallic Iris Blue - 261 beads
- #310 - Matte Black - 311 beads
- #233 - Lined Lustre Crystal Apricot - 305 beads

Star Rug

Back of
Sun Shines Woman

The back of Sun Shines Woman is a striking pattern in itself. Combining matte beads with glittering metallics gives the rug textural interest. You may want to use the design for both sides of a necklace bag. Whatever you choose, the result will be beautiful!

Indian Maiden Bead by Elaine LaFlex Green Gigglin' Grizzly Glass, gigglingrizzly@aol.com

Stitch: Peyote or Brick Size: Approximately 3" x 4" Beads: Delica

Begin Here - work Peyote Stitch beginning with this row. Work from left to right across the pattern.

For straps and embellishments, gather your own collection of beads, natural stones and crystals. Plan a design that makes the bag uniquely yours. Note: The bead quantities given do not include fringe and strap.

Sun Shines Woman

This pattern is slightly larger than the others in this book and so has its own back design. Add a small hook at the top, a longer strap and use it as a small shoulder bag! I accented mine with a handmade lampwork bead, but you could also accent this with various stones or other glass!

Stitch: Peyote or Brick　　Size: Approximately 3" x 4"　　Beads: Delica

Indian Maiden Bead
by Elaine LaFlex Green
Gigglin' Grizzly Glass,
Gigglingrizzly@aol.com

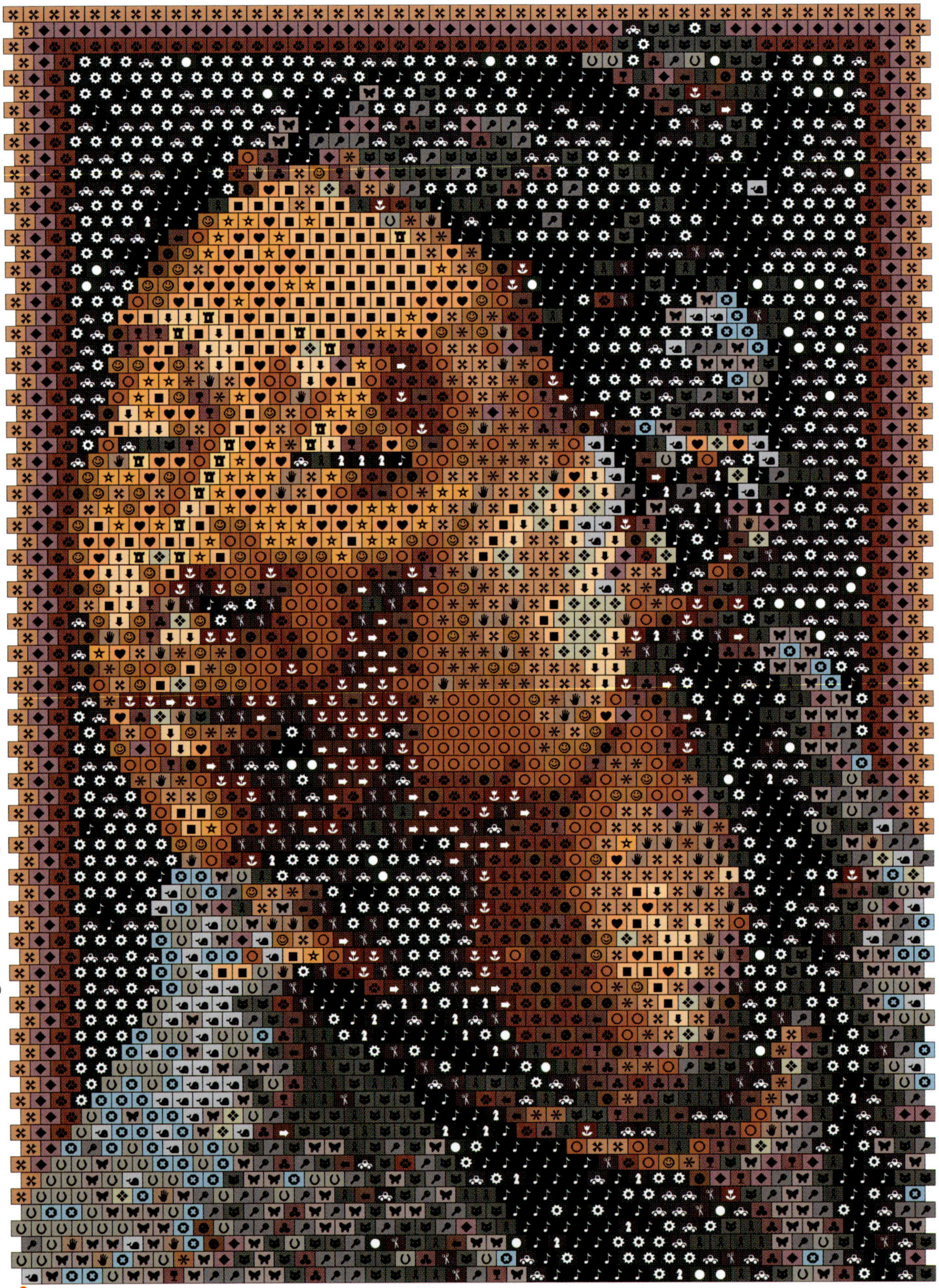

Begin Here - work Peyote Stitch beginning with this row. Work from left to right across the pattern.

For straps and embellishments, gather your own collection of beads, natural stones and crystals. Plan a design that makes the bag uniquely yours. Note: The bead quantities given do not include fringe and strap.

- #54 - Lined Rainbow Topaz Rose - 83 beads
- #69 - Lined Rainbow Crystal Tan - 79 beads
- #102 - Metallic Lustre Rose Gold - 163 beads
- #205 - Opaque Pearl Beige - 49 beads
- #208 - Opaque Tan - 99 beads
- #380 - Matte Metallic Lustre Green Pink - 40 beads
- #772 - Dyed Matte Transparent Mauve - 49 beads
- #853 - Matte Rainbow Transparent Dark Topaz - 54 beads
- #857 - Matte Rainbow Transparent Lt Amethyst - 448 beads
- #863 - Matte Rainbow Transparent Grey - 1278 beads
- #884 - Matte Opaque Rainbow Brown - 43 beads
- #230 - Lined Opalescent Crystal 24 kt Gold - 549 beads
- #242 - Transparent Pearl Grey - 83 beads
- #100 - Transparent Rainbow Light Topaz - 88 beads
- #702 - Transparent Light Topaz - 60 beads
- #256 - Lined Opaque Crystal Taupe - 55 beads
- #131 - Pink Lustre Moss Green - 41 beads
- #52 - Lined Rainbow Crystal Ivory - 40 beads
- #306 - Matte Opaque Gunmetal - 1159 beads
- #307 - Matte Opaque Grey - 142 beads
- #861 - Matte Rainbow Transparent Sky Blue - 145 beads
- #871 - Matte Opaque Rainbow Jet - 117 beads
- #865 - Matte Rainbow Transparent Smoke Topaz - 817 beads
- #882 - Matte Rainbow Opaque Grey - 87 beads
- #323 - Matte Metallic Iris Purple - 102 beads
- #202 - Pearl Rainbow White - 307 beads
- #734 - Opaque Chocolate Brown - 35 beads
- #287 - Lined Rainbow Light Topaz Lavender - 46 beads
- #773 - Dyed Matte Transparent Cherry - 65 beads
- #325 - Matte Metallic Iris Blue - 261 beads
- #310 - Matte Black - 311 beads
- #233 - Lined Lustre Crystal Apricot - 305 beads

- **#69** - Lined Rainbow Crystal Tan - 38 beads
- **#102** - Metallic Lustre Rose Gold - 90 beads
- **#203** - Opaque Pearl Light Yellow - 71 beads
- **#205** - Opaque Pearl Beige - 165 beads
- **#208** - Opaque Tan - 10 beads
- **#772** - Dyed Matte Transparent Mauve - 29 beads
- **#853** - Matte Rainbow Transparent Light Topaz - 50 beads
- **#857** - Matte Rainbow Transparent Light Amethyst - 17 bead
- **#883** - Matte Rainbow Opaque Ivory - 118 beads
- **#884** - Matte Opaque Rainbow Brown - 26 beads
- **#230** - Lined Opalescent Crystal 24 kt Gold - 60 beads
- **#100** - Transparent Rainbow Light Topaz - 10 beads
- **#321** - Matte Metallic Silver - 18 beads
- **#256** - Lined Opaque Crystal Taupe - 1 beads
- **#851** - Matte Rainbow Transparent Crystal - 23 beads
- **#52** - Lined Rainbow Crystal Ivory - 214 beads
- **#132** - Opaque Dark Grey Rainbow - 16 beads
- **#310** - Matte Opaque Black - 417 beads
- **#61** - Lined Rainbow Topaz Amethyst - 24 beads
- **#865** - Matte Rainbow Transparent Smoke Topaz - 26 beads
- **#323** - Matte Metallic Iris Purple - 55 beads
- **#769** - Matte Transparent Root Beer - 41 beads
- **#287** - Lined Rainbow Light Topaz Lavender - 30 beads
- **#325** - Matte Metallic Iris Blue - 274 beads
- **#280** - Lined Opaque Crystal Dark Plum - 28 beads
- **#110** - Transparent Rainbow Ice Blue - 125 beads
- **#111** - Transparent Rainbow Black Diamond - 103 beads
- **#114** - Transparent Lustre Silver Grey - 20 beads
- **#221** - Lined Metallic White Opal Gilt Lined - 151 beads

Bag by Deb Atkins, The Bead Hive, Wichita, KS 67213, 316-264-6616, D7442039@aol.com
Fringe, feathers & strap by Tina Napier, jnapier3@cox.net